Judaism:

Signs, Symbols, and Stories

Cath Senker

press.

New York

Published in 2010 by The Rosen Publishing Group Inc.
29 East 21st Street, New York, NY 10010

First Edition

Library of Congress Cataloging-in-Publication Data

Senker, Cath.
  Judaism: signs, symbols, stories / Cath Senker.
    p. cm. -- (Religious signs, symbols, and stories)
  Includes index.
  ISBN 978-1-4358-3039-4 (library binding)
  ISBN 978-1-4358-3047-9 (paperback)
  ISBN 978-1-4358-3055-4 (6-pack)
  1. Judaism--Juvenile literature. 1. Title.
  BM573.S46 2010
  296--dc22
                                    2008051912

0765
Manufactured in China

Disclaimer
Although every effort has been made to offer accurate and cle-arly expressed information, the author and publisher acknowledge
that some explanations may not be relevant to those who practice their faith in a different way.

Acknowledgements
The author and publisher would like to thank the following for allowing their pictures to be reproduced in this publication:
Cover illustrations: Roberto Tomei (front), Emmanuel Cerisier (back); Ask Images/ArkReligion.com: 20;
Bill Bachman/Alamy: 4T; Chris Fairclough: 8, 12 (both), 16, 18 (both), 19, 28; Clark & Ann Purcell/ Corbis: 4B; Helene
Rogers/ArkReligion.com: 10; Israel Images/Richard Nowitz/Alamy: 23; Itzhak Genut/Ark Religion.com: 24; Miriam Reik/Alamy:
22; Nir Alon/ Alamy: 21; Philippe Lissac/Panos Pictures: 14; Richard T. Nowitz/Corbis:11.

The author would like to thank the following for permission to reproduce material in this book: p.11 Poem from the Chasidic
mystical text Keter Shem Tov, translated in Your Word is Fire by Barry Holz and Arthur Green; p.15 From The Folk Literature of
the Kurdistani Jews: An Anthology by Yona Sabar; p.17 From Some Remarkable Stories about Mezuzos and Tefillin
(www.campsci.com); p.19 song from Hebrew songs (www.hebrewsongs.com); p.21 Poem from The New Jewish Baby Book;
p.23 poem by Roxanne Scher from (www.beingjewish.org).

With special thanks to Sam Horowitz.

The author and publisher would like to thank the following models: Celine Clark, Isobel Grace, Hari Johal, and Charlie Pengelly.

**Note to parents and teachers: The projects in this book are designed to be made by children. However, we do
recommend adult supervision at all times since the Publisher cannot be held responsible for any injury caused while
undertaking any activities.**

Contents

Activities

There are lots of activities throughout this book.

You can **read** stories, folk tales, and poems on pages 7, 11, 13, 15, 17, 21, 23, 29.

You can **sing** songs on page 19.

You can **make** traditional food on pages 25, 27.

You can **make** traditional crafts on pages 5, 9.

Signs and symbols

A sign usually has one clear meaning. Signs give important information. The emergency exit sign shows you where to go if a fire starts.

The Australian flag shows the seven-pointed star.

A symbol can have many meanings. Stars are often used as symbols. In daily life, stars may be given as a reward. If you do well, you might get a star on a chart.

There are different star shapes. The five-pointed star appears on the flags of several countries. The Israeli flag has a star with six points. This is the Jewish **Star of David**.

The Israeli flag has a six-pointed star.

Let's draw stars

Drawing stars

You will need a pen or pencil and some paper to draw your stars.

A six-pointed star

1. Draw a triangle with the base at the bottom.

2. Then draw a triangle the other way up over the top. It should be the same size.

3. The base of the second triangle should be one-third of the way down from the top of the first.

A five-pointed star

Keep your pencil on the paper until you have finished the star.

1. Draw an upside-down V.

2. Draw a line to cross the first line about one-third of the way up.

3. Draw a straight line to the right, crossing the other side of the V about one-third of the way down.

4. Draw a straight line back to your starting point.

The Star of David

The Star of David is the most common symbol of Judaism. It has six points because God protects the Jewish people from all six directions—north, south, east, west, up, and down. The six points of the star mean that God is protecting people everywhere and that they should put their trust in God. The Star of David is named after David, a king in the **Torah**, the Jewish Bible.

The Star of David is also called the Shield of David. It is named after King David, the second king of ancient Israel.

The Star of David was first used as a Jewish symbol in the Middle Ages. Under **Nazi** rule in World War II, Jewish people were forced to wear a yellow star to show they were Jews. Now, the Star of David is on the Israeli flag. It stands for the Jewish people and for the country of Israel. This shows that symbols can change their meaning over time.

The Shield of David

The Torah tells of a brave young shepherd boy named David. He took on the **Philistine** giant, Goliath, and killed him with a simple **catapult**. David became a skilled soldier and finally, the king of ancient Israel. This folk tale is about his shield.

A fearless soldier, David had his own special shield to protect him in battle. To save metal—which was expensive—his shield was not completely made of metal. Instead, it was formed from leather, stretched across a simple metal frame in the form of two triangles. The frame made a six-pointed star shape, which was very tough. David fought and won many battles using his shield. The star later became a symbol of the Jewish people.

The menorah

The **menorah** is a much earlier symbol of Judaism than the Star of David. Back in ancient times, the Jews had a **Temple** in Jerusalem. Inside, there was a large candle holder with seven branches, made from a single piece of gold. In each branch, there was a lamp burning olive oil.

The Temple was destroyed and rebuilt. After the Romans knocked it down a second time in 70 CE, the menorah disappeared. It was never made again, but it became a popular symbol of Judaism. In the twentieth century, the menorah became the symbol of the State of Israel.

*There is often a menorah in the **synagogue**, the Jewish place of worship. It symbolizes the menorah in the Temple.*

Let's make a menorah

A cardboard menorah

You will need:

6 toilet paper tubes and 1 longer tube, such as a kitchen paper tube. The tube in the center will be the tallest one.

Piece of cardboard or wood 16 inches (40 cm) long and 2.5 inches (6 cm) wide to form the base

Yellow or gold poster paint

Yellow and orange tissue paper

Tape, craft glue, and scissors

1. Cut down the longer tube so that it is about 2 inches (5 cm) taller than the other tubes.

2. Paint the cardboard tubes and allow them to dry.

3. Tape the tubes to the base.

4. Cut out flame shapes from tissue paper and glue or stick them to the tops of the cardboard tubes.

Ner tamid

In the Torah, God commanded the Jewish people to create an **eternal** light. In **Hebrew**, it is called a **ner tamid**. The everlasting light reminded the Jewish people that God would always be there to help them. In the ancient Temple, the oil in the menorah was kept burning constantly.

Today, a light called the ner tamid burns in every synagogue in the world. It stands for the menorah. Some say the light reminds Jewish people that everyone has a spark of holy fire inside them and can spread holiness in the world.

You can see the ner tamid near the top of this photograph of a synagogue.

Poem about the ner tamid

When you focus all your thought
On the power of the words of prayer
You may begin to see the sparks of light that shine within them.
The sacred letters are the chambers [enclosed spaces]
Into which God pours His flowing light.
The lights within each letter, as they touch,
Ignite one another [set one another on fire],
And new lights are born.
It is of this that the Psalmist [writer of biblical poems] says:
Light is sown for the righteous [good people], and joy for the
upright in heart!

The Torah

During worship in the synagogue, Jewish people read from the Torah. The Torah is written by hand in Hebrew on special scrolls. It is treated with great respect.

The Jewish people believe that the Torah contains God's words. In it, God speaks directly to them. He also uses many signs and symbols to communicate with them. When God first wished to appear to the Jewish people at **Mount Sinai**, he sent thunder and lightning, clouds of smoke, and trumpet music as signs that he was coming to visit them on earth.

Out of respect, no one touches the Torah.

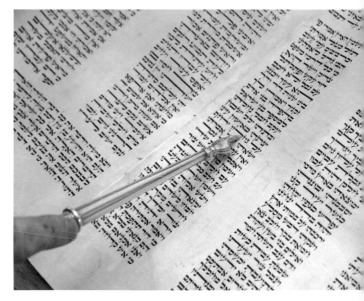

People point to the words of the Torah with a pointer called a yad.

Let's read the Torah

The burning bush

The Jewish people were slaves in Egypt, doing back-breaking work for no reward. In despair, they called on God to help them.

One day, a Jewish man named Moses saw an amazing sight. A bush was burning, but was not destroyed by the flames. It was a sign from God. When Moses came closer, God spoke to him. "Moses, you must lead the Jews out of slavery in Egypt," he said. "No one will believe this is possible!" cried Moses. God replied, "I will give you the power to perform three miracles. Then the people will believe in you."

First, Moses threw his walking stick to the ground. It turned into a snake! Then he placed his hand on his chest, and it became white with the disease **leprosy**. *He did it again, and the disease went away. Finally, Moses poured a bucket of water on the ground, and it turned to blood. The Jews knew that these miracles were a sign from God. They were ready to follow Moses.*

13

The tzizit, tallit, and tefillin

These worshipers wear a tallit, tefillin and kippah to pray.

Some Jewish people (mostly men) wear symbolic clothing to help them remember God when they are worshiping. They wear a four-cornered shawl called a **tallit**, with fringes called **tzizit**. The tzizit remind them of the Jewish laws they must follow.

Jewish men also wear **tefillin** for weekday morning prayers. Tefillin are little leather pouches that contain verses from the Torah. People wear them on their left arm facing the heart, and on their forehead, to remember to love God with all their heart and their mind.

Men and boys also wear a cap called a **kippah**. It is a sign of respect to God.

Poor but generous

There once lived a very poor man and his wife. She had just given birth to a baby. They didn't even have any clothing to wrap the baby in. That day, a stranger appeared. "My wife has just had a baby," the poor man said. "We do not even have straw to lay him upon." The couple, poor though they were, gave the stranger some straw. He filled his tallit with straw and left. When he was out of sight, he threw down the straw.

The following morning, the husband went outside. There on the ground was a pile of silver and gold coins. He realized that the stranger was none other than the **Prophet Elijah.** *Elijah had turned the straw into riches to reward the couple for their kindness.*

The mezuzah

The **mezuzah** is a small piece of **parchment** with two verses from the Torah on it. The verses are carefully written by an expert and must always be perfect. They say there is one God, who promises to look after the Jewish people if they follow his rules.

Some Jewish people touch the mezuzah when they pass it, and then kiss their fingers.

The mezuzah is placed inside a metal or wooden case. A mezuzah is attached to the doorpost of every room of a Jewish home except the bathroom.

The mezuzah reminds Jewish people that they should serve God in everything they do. It is also a symbol of God's promise to the Jews to protect them.

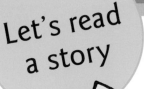

It's all in the mezuzah

A young Jewish boy was suffering from terrible headaches and a sharp pain in the eyes. The eye doctor told him he needed to have an operation immediately, or he would lose his sight in one eye.

*Naturally, the boy was extremely upset. His father decided to visit the **rabbi**. The rabbi said, "Check the mezuzah outside your son's room." The father took the mezuzah to an expert. To his amazement, the expert discovered it had a mistake in it. The boy's father quickly went out to buy a new, perfect one.*

The following day, he took his son to the hospital for a checkup before the operation. The doctor was surprised to see that the eye was slightly better, and decided not to operate. A week passed, and the eye healed completely.

Shabbat

Shabbat is the Jewish day of rest. It lasts from Friday at sunset until nightfall on Saturday. Just before sunset, the mother of the family lights two candles as a sign that Shabbat has started. The two candles symbolize knowing the laws of Shabbat and obeying them.

*The mother lights the Shabbat candle and says a **blessing**.*

The father says blessings over wine and two **challot** (special braided loaves). Wine is a symbol of the holiness of Shabbat. The challot are a reminder of the food God provided to the Jews while they were wandering in the desert after escaping from Egypt.

The father of the family blesses the wine.

Let's sing
a song

Shabbat

Come my beloved, to
meet the bride [the
Shabbat],
Let us welcome the
Shabbat.
And Dad trills his voice
in Shabbat songs
freedom calls on son and daughter.

And a white tablecloth is set and candles are lit
and like an echo from the past, the melodies repeat
and the house is suddenly filled with those songs.

Come my beloved, to meet the bride,
The Shabbat Queen here she rises
The challa [braided loaf] is on the table and prayer rises
all the house dwellers sing in a great choir.

Dad's lips whisper and his eyes are as lights
and like an echo from the past, the melodies repeat
and the house is suddenly filled with those songs.

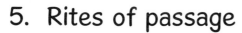
Circumcision and naming ceremonies

During **circumcision** (*Brit Milah* in Hebrew), a trained person removes the **foreskin** of a baby boy's penis. It is a symbol of becoming a member of the Jewish people.

After the circumcision, the family often holds a party to celebrate.

In the Torah, God told Abraham, the first Jew, that all boys should be circumcised as a symbol of the agreement between God and the Jewish people. God promised to look after the Jews if they followed his laws.

Baby girls are given their names in the synagogue on the Shabbat after they are born. Outside Israel, most babies have both a Jewish name for religious ceremonies and a nonreligious name for daily life.

Let's read
a poem

For a Brit Milah

How shall we bless him?

With what will this child be blessed?

With a smile like light.

With eyes large and wide, to see every flower, animal, and bird,

and a heart to feel all he sees.

Bat and Bar Mitzvah

Bar Mitzvah means "son of the **commandment**" (Jewish law). When a boy reaches 13, he becomes Bar Mitzvah. He is now a Jewish adult. Girls become **Bat Mitzvah** at 12.

These twins read from the Torah at their Bat and Bar Mitzvah ceremonies.

After they become Bar or Bat Mitzvah, children should follow the Jewish laws like adults and take part in religious services.

Boys have a Bar Mitzvah ceremony in the synagogue as a symbol that they have come of age. Some girls celebrate their Bat Mitzvah in the synagogue, too. At the ceremony, the young person comes to the platform to say a blessing from the Torah. Today, some young women as well as men wear a tallit, as a sign that they are adults in Jewish law.

Tallis

This young woman describes wearing her tallis (tallit) as an adult in the synagogue:

I murmur the blessing
before flinging it on,
my silky, rippling tallis.
Like a whispering breath
on my shoulders, it reminds me
that I will now be praying.
The knotted fringes twine
around my fingers, like
ropes pulling me to safety.
Lilac and purple, blue and
turquoise, it catches the light
and sunlight splashes onto me.

Waves of fabric roll onto
my arms,
stroking my neck with
their flowing fingertips.
I touch the knot to
the Torah as it goes by,
then kiss it with pride.
My silky, rippling tallis.

By Roxanne Scher

Passover

Every year at **Passover**, Jewish families remember the ancient story of the Jews' escape from slavery in Egypt to Israel. The Jews were in a great hurry to leave, but they needed food for the long journey. There was no time for their bread to rise, so they made flat crackers called **matzah**.

Jewish people clean their dishes to get rid of chametz in preparation for Passover.

During Passover, Jewish people eat matzah as a symbol of the escape from Egypt. They don't eat any **chametz**—foods such as bread and cakes that rise when baked. Also, these foods are a symbol of pride because they become "puffed up." Jewish people do not eat chametz to show they are humble, not proud.

Let's make matzah

Recipe for matzah

Ask an adult to help you bake

You will need:

4 cups all-purpose flour
1 teaspoon salt
3/4 cup sunflower oil
3/4 cup water
(add more if needed)

1. Preheat the oven to 350° F (180° C).

2. Spread a little oil on a baking sheet.

3. Mix the salt into the flour.

4. Add the oil and knead it into the flour.

5. Gradually add the water and knead it into the dough until it is no longer sticky.

6. Flatten the dough with a rolling pin until it is 1/2 inch (1cm) thick. Shape it so it will fit in the baking sheet.

7. Put the dough in the baking sheet. Cut it into squares.

8. Bake in the oven for 15–20 minutes, until crispy.

Seder night

On the first night of the Passover festival, Jewish families gather for **Seder** night. They tell the story of the Jews' escape from Egypt. There are many symbols to bring the story to life.

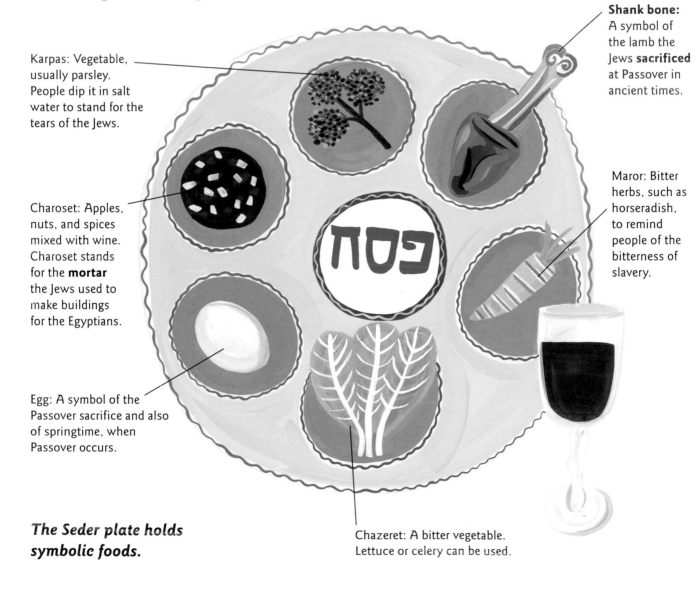

Shank bone: A symbol of the lamb the Jews **sacrificed** at Passover in ancient times.

Karpas: Vegetable, usually parsley. People dip it in salt water to stand for the tears of the Jews.

Charoset: Apples, nuts, and spices mixed with wine. Charoset stands for the **mortar** the Jews used to make buildings for the Egyptians.

Maror: Bitter herbs, such as horseradish, to remind people of the bitterness of slavery.

Egg: A symbol of the Passover sacrifice and also of springtime, when Passover occurs.

The Seder plate holds symbolic foods.

Chazeret: A bitter vegetable. Lettuce or celery can be used.

Let's make Seder

Recipe for charoset

Ask an adult to help you to cut the apples

You will need:

2 apples, unpeeled

1 cup ground walnuts

1 teaspoon cinnamon

3 tablespoons red grape juice (adults would use sweet Passover wine)

honey or sugar to taste

1. Chop up the apples. You can use a food processor.

2. Add the rest of the ingredients and mix well.

3. Keep the charoset in the refrigerator until it is needed. It's best to eat it within two hours!

Hanukkah

At Hanukkah, Jewish people remember the miracle of the oil in the Temple that lasted for eight days. The festival lasts

The ninth candle is the servant candle. It is used to light the other candles.

for eight days. Each night, Jews light candles on a **hanukiah**, a nine-branched menorah. On the first night they light one candle, on the second night two, and so on until all eight candles are burning brightly.

During the festival, people eat foods cooked in oil, another symbol of the miracle. They eat doughnuts and **latke**—tasty fried potato cakes.

Hanukkah

In the second century BCE, the Greek-Syrian king, Antiochus IV, ruled over a vast empire, including ancient Israel. He tried to force everyone in his empire to adopt the Greek way of life. Antiochus told the Jews they could not keep their Shabbat and had to worship Greek gods.

Many of the Jews refused. Led by Judah Maccabee, they rose up and bravely fought Antiochus' troops. In 164 BCE, they conquered Jerusalem. The Jews found their beloved holy Temple in ruins. It was filthy and there was garbage everywhere. First, they searched for oil to relight the ner tamid. They found only a small bottle, enough to burn for one day. God worked a miracle and made the oil last for eight days.

Bar Mitzvah The term for a boy when he reaches 13 and becomes a Jewish adult.

Bat Mitzvah The term for a girl when she reaches 12 and becomes a Jewish adult.

blessing A prayer asking for God's help and protection.

catapult A weapon used for throwing stones.

challot (plural of challah) The two loaves of braided bread that are eaten at the Shabbat meal.

chametz Foods that rise when they are cooked and cannot be eaten during Passover.

circumcision Cutting off the foreskin from the penis.

commandment Religious law.

eternal Lasting forever.

foreskin The skin over the tip of the penis.

hanukiah A nine-branched candle holder that is lit during Hanukkah.

Hebrew The Jewish holy language. The Torah and prayer books are written in Hebrew.

kippah A small cap that Jewish men and boys wear when they pray or study Judaism.

latkes Latkes are like little burgers, made from shredded potato and fried.

leprosy An infectious disease that causes painful white areas on the skin and can destroy nerves and flesh.

matzah A flat cracker made from flour and water.

menorah A seven-branched candle holder. It is an ancient Jewish symbol.

mezuzah A special piece of paper with important words from the Torah written on it. It is kept in a case and fixed to a doorframe.

mortar A mixture that is used in building for holding bricks and stones together.

Mount Sinai A mountain in Egypt.

Nazi The Nazis were the German party that ruled Germany from 1933 to 1945 and tried to kill all the Jews in Europe.

ner tamid Light that burns forever.

parchment A thin material made from the skin of a sheep or goat. In the past, people used it for writing on. It is used to make mezuzahs.

Passover The eight-day festival when Jewish people remember the Jews' escape from slavery in Egypt.

Philistine One of the Philistines, a people who settled in what is now Israel and Palestine at around the same time as the Jews. According to the Torah, the Philistines fought the Jews until King David defeated them.

Prophet Elijah A Jewish prophet, a person sent by God to teach people how to live the right way.

rabbi A Jewish religious leader and teacher.

sacrificed To be given as an offering to God (usually an animal).

Seder A festive meal at the start of Passover. Jewish people tell the story of the escape from Egypt using symbols.

Shabbat The Jewish day of rest, from sunset on Friday until nightfall on Saturday.

shank bone A bone from the shin of a lamb, used on the Seder plate. Sometimes a chicken bone is used instead.

Star of David The six-pointed star that is a symbol of Judaism.

synagogue The Jewish place of worship and learning.

tallit A shawl with four corners that men wear for the morning service in the synagogue.

tefillin Two little leather pouches with verses from the Torah. Jewish men tie one to the arm and one to the head for the morning service in synagogue.

Temple The Jewish place of worship in ancient Jerusalem.

Torah The Jewish Bible. It includes the first five books of the Christian Bible, plus two books called Prophets and Holy Writings.

tzizit The fringes on the corner of a tallit. They remind people of the Jewish laws.

Books to read

Celebrate Hanukkah: With Lights, Latkes, and Dreidels
by Deborah Heiligman (National Geographic Children's Books, 2008)

Holiday Stories: The Passover Story
by Anita Ganeri (Smart Apple Media, 2004)

Keystones: Jewish Synagogue
by Laurie Rosenberg (Topeka Bindery, 2000)

Menorahs, Mezuzas, and Other Jewish Symbols
by Miriam Chaikin (Sandpiper, 2003)

My Jewish Year
by Cath Senker (Powerkids Press, 2007)

What You Will See Inside A Synagogue
by Lawrence A Hoffman (Skylight Paths Publishing, 2008)

Web Sites

Due to the changing nature of Internet links, PowerKids Press has developed an online list of Web sites related to the subject of this book. This site is updated regularly. Please use this link to access this list:
www.powerkidslinks.com/sss/judaism